I Know Someone with
HIV/AIDS

Elizabeth Raum

www.raintreepublishers.co.uk
Visit our website to find out
more information about
Raintree books.

To order:

☎ Phone 0845 6044371

📄 Fax +44 (0) 1865 312263

💻 Email myorders@raintreepublishers.co.uk

Customers from outside the UK please telephone +44 1865 312262

Raintree is an imprint of Capstone Global Library
Limited, a company incorporated in England and
Wales having its registered office at 7 Pilgrim Street,
London, EC4V 6LB – Registered company number:
6695582

Text © Capstone Global Library Limited 2011
First published in hardback in 2011
The moral rights of the proprietor have been asserted.

Edited by Rebecca Rissman, Dan Nunn,
  and Catherine Veitch
Designed by Steve Mead and Joanna Hinton Malivoire
Picture research by Tracy Cummins
Originated by Capstone Global Library
Printed and bound in China by Leo Paper Products Ltd

ISBN 978 1 406 22082 7
15 14 13 12 11
10 9 8 7 6 5 4 3 2 1

British Library Cataloguing in Publication Data
Raum, Elizabeth.
I know someone with HIV/AIDS. – (Understanding
health issues)
616.9'792-dc22
A full catalogue record for this book is available from
the British Library.

Acknowledgements
We would like to thank the following for permission to
reproduce photographs: Corbis pp. **7** (© David Scharf/
Science Faction), **8** (© Image Source), **10** (© Gareth
Brown), **12** (© Edith Held), **14** (© Jim Craigmyle), **15** (©
Simon Jarratt), **29** (© Tetra Image); Getty Images pp. **16**
(Joe Raedle), **21** (Flynn Larsen), **22** (Stuart O'Sullivan),
24 (Commercial Eye), **26** (Nathaniel S. Butler/NBAE),
27 (Kevin Winter); Heinemann Raintree p. **20** (Richard
Huchingson); istockphoto pp **4** (© Chris Schmidt), **6**
(© Andrew Rich), **9** (© Rosemarie Gearhart), **18** (©
onebluelight); Photo Researchers, Inc. p. **11** (Mauro
Fermariello); Shutterstock pp. **5** (© ZouZou), **17** (©
Greenland), **25** (© wow).

Cover photograph of college students on campus
reproduced with permission of Corbis (Corbis Yellow).

We would like to thank Ashley Wolinski and Matthew
Siegel for their invaluable help in the preparation of
this book.

Every effort has been made to contact copyright
holders of any material reproduced in this book. Any
omissions will be rectified in subsequent printings if
notice is given to the publisher.

All the Internet addresses (URLs) given in this book
were valid at the time of going to press. However, due
to the dynamic nature of the Internet, some addresses
may have changed, or sites may have changed or
ceased to exist since publication. While the author and
publisher regret any inconvenience this may cause
readers, no responsibility for any such changes can be
accepted by either the author or the publisher.

Contents

Some words are printed in bold, **like this**. You can find out what they mean in the glossary.

Do you Know someone with HIV/AIDS?

Have you heard about HIV/AIDS before? It is a disease that can make people very ill. HIV stands for **Human Immunodeficiency Virus**, and AIDS stands for **Acquired Immune Deficiency Syndrome**.

HIV can affect anyone.

You can't tell if people have HIV just by looking at them.

Many people with HIV are adults or teenagers. Some children have HIV, too. You might know someone with HIV/AIDS.

What is HIV/AIDS?

The human body is made up of trillions of **cells**. Some cells fight off diseases. Some of these cells are called **T-cells**.

T-cells are like superheroes. They fight disease.

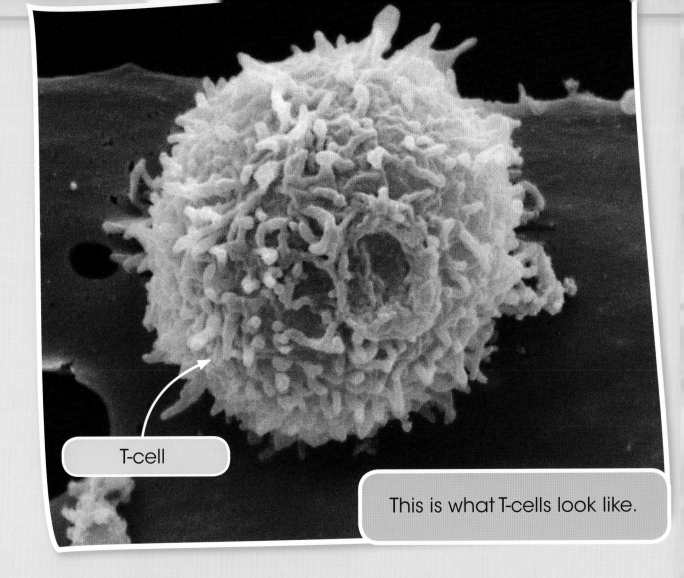

T-cell

This is what T-cells look like.

HIV is an illness that attacks the T-cells that fight disease. When there are not enough cells to fight HIV, doctors say that the person has AIDS.

Mothers and babies

Most children who have HIV were born with it. Their mothers passed it on when they were **pregnant** or during childbirth.

Today doctors test pregnant women for HIV.

Today, many pregnant women are tested for HIV. If they have it, doctors give them special medicine that protects their babies.

Many babies can be protected from HIV if people get the right help, at the right time.

Blood and HIV

One of the ways people can get HIV is through the blood of someone who has HIV. If someone with a cut on their hand touches the blood of someone with HIV, the virus can spread to them from the other person.

If a friend gets injured and is bleeding, ask an adult to help them.

You cannot get HIV from touching your own blood.

Blood may carry other diseases, too. For this reason, you should never touch anyone else's blood. If you see a friend bleeding, it is a good idea to tell an adult.

Will I get HIV?

You cannot get HIV by hugging a friend.

You can't get HIV by playing with your friends at school. You can't get it by sharing a biscuit or swimming in the same pool.

You can't get HIV from insect bites or pets. You can't catch it like a cold. Even if a person with HIV coughs or sneezes near you, you won't catch HIV.

You can't get HIV from:
- touching someone with HIV
- hugging someone with HIV
- kissing someone with HIV
- sharing food or drink with someone who has HIV
- shaking hands
- using the same swimming pool
- using the same toilet.

Living with HIV

There is no **cure** for HIV. People who have HIV must take medicine for the rest of their lives.

This scientist is making medicines for people with HIV.

These people are walking to raise money for AIDS **research**.

The medicine helps the **T-cells** in the body to keep fighting HIV for longer. Medicines help people with HIV live a longer, healthier life.

Fighting illness

Adults and children with HIV find it difficult to fight off illnesses. They may become very ill when they have a cold or an ear **infection**. They have to be careful to avoid such illnesses.

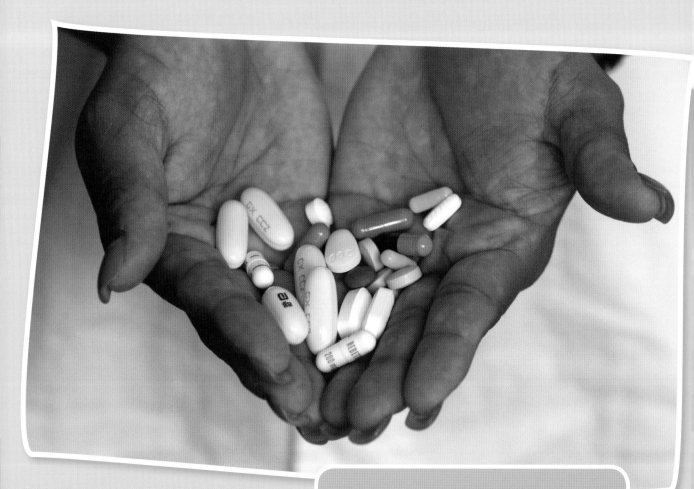

Most people with HIV must take medicine every day.

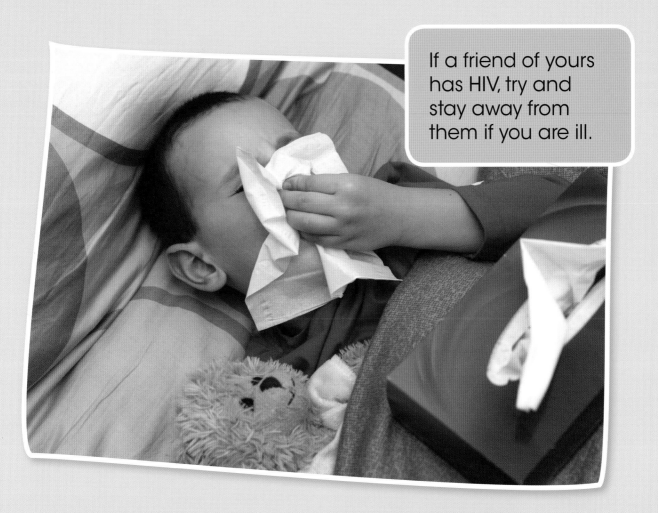

If a friend of yours has HIV, try and stay away from them if you are ill.

It can be very easy to spread **germs** from one person to another. If you are ill, try to keep away from your friends until you feel better.

Wash your hands with soap and water for at least 20 seconds.

It is important that people with HIV get flu injections and take their medicine to help them keep well. You can help to stop colds and flu from spreading to others by washing your hands often.

Tips for washing your hands:
- use soap and warm water
- scrub for at least 20 seconds (if you don't have a clock, sing the ABC song)
- scrub front and back, under your fingernails, and between your fingers
- dry with a clean towel or paper towel.

Keeping healthy

Some children with HIV may have a hard time gaining weight. For others, HIV medicines may make them put on weight. It's important that children with HIV eat a healthy diet.

All children should eat fresh fruit and vegetables.

Sleep helps the body fight disease.

Every child should have a healthy diet. Fresh fruit, vegetables, wholegrains, and lean meat give us energy and help us stay strong. It's also important for everyone to exercise every day and get enough sleep every night.

Being a friend

Everyone needs friends. Children with HIV may feel lonely. They may be afraid to tell others that they have HIV. They may worry that other children will stay away from them.

These friends are enjoying doing a puzzle together.

Ways to have fun with your friend:

- put on a play or show
- draw or paint
- do craft projects
- put puzzles together
- play board games
- build with building blocks
- hold doll fashion shows
- race toy cars
- ride bicycles
- read together.

But you know you cannot catch HIV by being near someone. You can be with them without worrying about HIV. Listening to music and working on projects together are great ways to show you care.

Helping at home

Children with HIV often have a parent who has HIV, too. Your friend may have to help care for other members of the family. It is also possible that your friend lives with a grandparent or other relative.

Helping each other with jobs makes life easier.

Friends enjoy time together at school.

Your friend may not want to talk about what is happening at home. Your friend may not be able to invite you over. A good friend understands.

Famous people

Magic Johnson is one of the greatest players in basketball history. In 1991, he learned that he had HIV. Magic Johnson still has HIV, but new medicines have helped him to stay healthy.

Magic Johnson played basketball for the Los Angeles Lakers in the United States.

Magic Johnson helps teenagers to understand HIV.

Today, Magic talks to teenagers about how to prevent HIV. He also raises money to help people who have HIV/AIDS and to help doctors find a **cure**.

The truth about HIV/AIDS

You can catch HIV by hugging and kissing someone who has it.

FALSE! HIV is not like a cold. You cannot catch it by touching someone or breathing the same air.

You can catch HIV by swimming in a public pool or using a public toilet.

FALSE! You cannot even catch HIV by using the same cup or spoon.

Everyone who has HIV will get AIDS.

FALSE! New medicines help to prevent AIDS. People with HIV are living longer and healthier lives.

Glossary

Acquired Immune Deficiency Syndrome disease that makes it hard for the body to fight other illnesses

cell smallest unit that makes up living things

cure medical treatment that makes someone better

germs tiny living things that can cause disease

Human Immunodeficiency Virus virus that attacks the cells that fight disease and makes people more likely to get ill

infection an illness. Germs cause infections.

pregnant expecting a baby

research investigate something to find out more information about it

T-cells cells in the body that fight off diseases

Find out more

Books to read

Kids' Kitchen, Fiona Bird (Barefoot Books, 2009)

World's Worst Germs, Anna Claybourne
  (Raintree, 2006)

Websites

**http://kidshealth.org/kid/stay_healthy/
index.html**
Learn about health and safety.

**http://kidshealth.org/parent/infections/std/
hiv.html**
Find out about HIV and AIDS.

Index